STAMP IT!

STAMP IT!

A Project Book of Stamp Pad Prints and Patterns

Kay Gleason

VNR **Van Nostrand Reinhold Company**
New York Cincinnati Toronto London Melbourne

Photographs by Batista Moon Studio/Gallery
Designed by Gayle Jaeger

Published by Van Nostrand Reinhold Company
135 West 50th Street, New York, NY 10020

Van Nostrand Reinhold Limited
1410 Birchmount Road
Scarborough, Ontario M1P 2E7, Canada

Van Nostrand Reinhold Australia Pty. Ltd.
17 Queen Street
Mitcham, Victoria 3132, Australia

Van Nostrand Reinhold Company Limited
Molly Millars Lane
Wokingham, Berkshire, England

16 15 14 13 12 11 10 9 8 7 6 5 4 3 2 1

Library of Congress Cataloging in Publication Data

Gleason, Kay.
  Stamp it!
  Includes index.
  1. Rubber stamp printing. I. Title.
TT867.G56   761   81-2114
ISBN 0-442-26161-6   AACR2

Contents

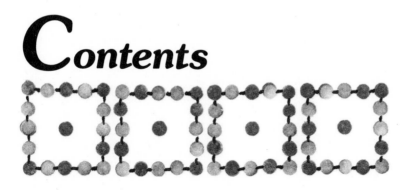

Introduction

The world surrounds us with pleasing patterns. Geese in flight, ivy leaves against a wall, and ripples on a pond all have an appeal that comes from the repetition of a single shape.

The pleasure that the rhythms of repeated shapes bring inspires us not only to admire them, but to create our own as well. We all experience pattern formation of some kind . . . the builder chooses his chimney stones carefully, the hostess arranges her candles and crystal, a child pats dimples in the roadside dust.

Stamp pads—familiar, inexpensive, and readily available—provide a medium for more conscious pattern formation. A printing process that is simple and satisfying encourages the development of patterns, and stamp pad printing is ideal for this purpose.

Even a small child enjoys stamping prints. He makes his mark with enthusiasm, his patterns are spontaneous, and planning is not needed. An older child will stamp more carefully, observing the effects of different arrangements. Assorted printing supplies kept available in the home or classroom can help encourage interest in pattern and appreciation of design. Children too young to cut their own stamps can produce successful and highly original designs by using stamps cut for them. Though some children want direction, most do best when left alone, to learn the feel of the materials and procedure, and then to begin trying possibilities here such as those suggested.

An adult using the same materials and procedures will of course bring them to his own level of sophistication and adapt them to his preferred style. Stamp pad prints have long been used by fabric designers to help visualize an overall expanse of repeats. These can be as dramatic and bold as primitive art or as complex as intertwining florals.

For some, the pleasure alone of stamp pad printing justifies its pursuit; for others, stamp pad printing may lead to a serious involvement in the field of design. For everyone, it is hoped that the ideas presented here will intensify the enjoyment of patterns everywhere while opening new avenues for self-expression.

CHAPTER ONE

Pattern formation and printing techniques

A limitless array of design possibilities is literally at your fingertips. With an assortment of just a few simple materials you can experience the enjoyment of printing your own patterns. See for yourself. Assemble a stamp pad and ink, assorted erasers, a single-edged razor blade, some paper, and you will be ready to go.

When you have made yourself comfortable, choose an eraser, stamp it on the pad to ink it, and then stamp it in as many different arrangements as you can on a piece of paper. Do not concern yourself at first with keeping lines straight or with trying to complete a perfect design. Experiment. Challenge yourself to see how many ways one shape can be printed, then try combining it with other shapes. Build a pattern of large shapes, then add smaller ones in some or all of the spaces.

Now take your single-edged razor blade and alter the eraser shapes. A line or notch in an eraser will completely change the kinds of patterns it will make. Cut some of your erasers in half. Cut clean, shallow lines or notches in the print-

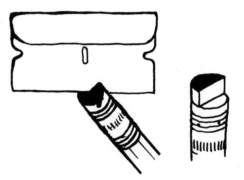

• **Use a single-edged razor blade to create a stamp from a pencil eraser.**

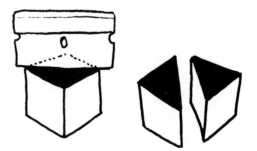

• **Erasers can be cut into countless shapes with a single-edged razor blade.**

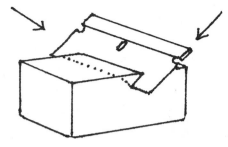

• **To carve a shallow strip from an eraser surface, hold the razor blade at an angle. Slant the cuts toward each other for easy removal of the cut area.**

ing surface of others. Always angle the blade so that the cuts slant inward toward each other, undercutting the piece to be lifted out and removed. See the illustration. Keep the beginning cuts simple and limit them to straight lines.

Now that you have a variety of shapes, try experimenting with each cut shape to see what the single unit looks like in repeat. Pin practice sheets on the wall and take time to notice which arrangements look best to you. Save these sheets of pattern sketches and use them as a source of ideas when you are ready to print a completely developed design of your own.

Design units and networks
A *design unit* is the figure that forms the main element of a pattern. The illustration shows some of the basic shapes used as design units in patterns—the square, diamond, circle, triangle, and octagon. Each

• **Basic shapes of design units—square, diamond, circle, triangle, octagon.**

of these shapes can be repeated in a variety of arrangements. Striped patterns with prints repeated in vertical or horizontal rows evolve most easily.

The guidelines upon which pattern shapes are arranged are called *networks*. The square network exemplified by graph paper is the one most familiar to us. The illustrations show others. The half-drop or brick network, and the diamond, triangle, and hexagon networks are also common.

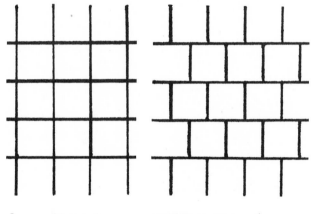

Square Network   **Half-Drop Network**

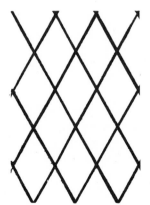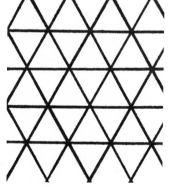

Diamond Network   **Triangle Network**

• **Common networks—square, brick, diamond, triangle.**

Curved lines form scale and ogee networks. In each of these networks, lines divide the area into spaces that are all the same size and the same shape.

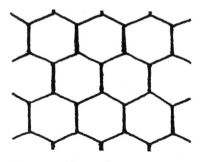

Hexagon Network

Scale Network

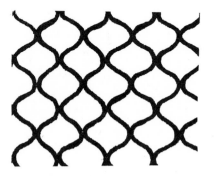

Ogee Network

• **Additional familiar networks—hexagon, scale, ogee.**

• **Prints within a visible brick (or half-drop) network and an invisible brick network.**

A pattern can either be organized with a visible network that becomes part of the design or with an invisible network, as when a penciled network is erased after printing is completed. The illustration shows both. In some patterns, parts of the invisible network are left unprinted. These windowlike spaces form their own secondary patterns, as you can see in the illustration on page 12.

11

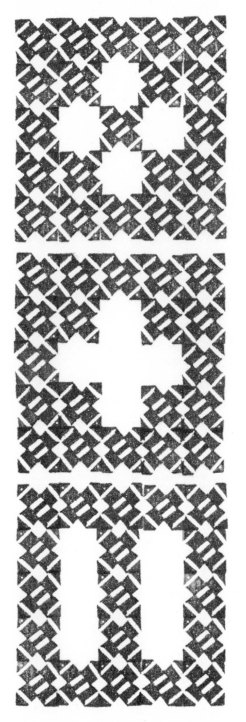

Use a felt marker and ruler to make a collection of large-sized networks of all kinds. You can then use these under lightweight paper as an aid in design formation, and they will encourage you to engage in a wider range of pattern exploration. Graph paper with concentric circles and radiating lines, as well as paper with triangular graphs, can be purchased at stationery stores where engineering supplies are carried. These papers are helpful as guides for developing small patterns.

Spacing

You can dramatically alter patterns by changing the amount of space allowed be-

• A pattern with parts of the network left unprinted to form a windowlike central design.

• Variations in spacing between square design units dramatically change a pattern.

tween design units. Even the slightest change in the spacing can make one pattern quite different from another, as the illustration shows. When no space is left between design units, only the cut areas form the pattern. When space is left between units, however, the unprinted space itself becomes an additional element in the design. With wider spaces separating the units, each unit is seen as an individual design, as well as a part of the pattern.

Rotating

As the illustration shows, when some kinds of design units are printed in four-step rotation, the print units form another whole. This is the result with design units carved in cornerlike arrangements (top, left in illustration), diagonal arrangements (top, right), and arrangements that seem to emanate from one corner.

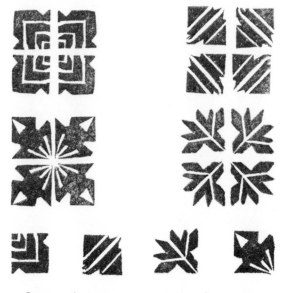

• **Square design units printed in four-step rotation.**

You can also use stamps in half-turn rotation as pairs, as well as in groups of four, for interesting results.

Wedge-shaped stamps make interesting designs when worked in rotation. As the illustration shows, you can arrange them as in the slices of a pie, or print them radiating from a small central print. These designs, which might have the look of snowflakes or daisies, will resemble traditional sunburst patterns if you leave space in the center of the circle and reverse the prints to point outward.

• **Wedge-shaped design units pointing outward around a circle, and inward around a small print, printed in rotation.**

Counterchanging

The illustration shows the interesting result of using positive and negative versions of the same design unit. To experiment with this concept, stamp an inked, carved eraser on the surface of a clean, uncarved eraser. Using a single-edged razor blade, cut away only the printed areas. The second

• **A counterchange pattern: positive and negative images of the same design unit printed alternately.**

eraser will now print a negative version of the first. Print the two in alternate spaces. The result is a counterchange pattern.

14

Reflecting

For some patterns composed of asymmetrical design units, you may want a mirror-image print as a companion piece. Ink a carved eraser stamp, and then print it on an uncut clean eraser. Carve away the unprinted areas of the second eraser. It will then print as a reflection of the original.

• A reflection pattern is one that consists of design units and their mirror images. Two stamps were used for each leaf in this pattern in order to print one-half of the leaf darker (or in a different color) than the other. The stamp for the leaf's right side was inked for each printing, stamped on scrap paper to remove some ink, then printed.

15

Branching patterns
Vertical stripes of wavy lines can be treated as stems sprouting leaves and flowers. Other floral design units, such as the one illustrated, use meandering branched lines that extend to all four sides of the stamp. The lines or stems are designed to touch opposite margins at the

• **A continuous pattern of S-shaped stems with leaves and berries.**

same point and same degree of slant so that, when printed, the stem will have the look of continuous growth throughout the pattern.

16

• Sketch of a floral design unit with branching stems extending to all four sides.

• Print made with an adhesive foam stamp; a simplified version of the sketch in the illustration shown left.

To plan this type of design unit, pencil sketch branching lines on a square piece of graph paper. Have some branching lines touch opposite edges of the paper. Lay the sketch facedown and fold the top third of the paper back and down, creasing it horizontally. Fold the lower third up, so the two edges meet at the center. Erase and redraw any penciled lines that do not meet perfectly at the seam. Unfold the paper and repeat the process with the two side sections, folding them back to make adjustments in the location of lines. Try this yourself by tracing the branching design in the illustration. The lines will meet when folded. You can also check the accuracy of the "joins" in a design unit by curving it around a rolled piece of paper.

Interlacing

Wherever two lines cross in a design unit or pattern, one can be made to look as if it is passing over the other. This is *interlacement*. Plan interlaced designs with pencil sketches of units with a band (a double line) that crosses another band. Erasing the crossed portion of one band will make it look as if it is covered by the other. The illustrations show interlaced bands and circles.

• **Interlacement of crossed bands. A slight change in the basic design unit dramatically changes the kinds of patterns it prints.**

Crossed bands in repeat become a basketweave pattern. When the same stamp is printed in rotation one entire grid seems to rest on another. Areas of straight prints can be combined with rotated prints for a more complex pattern.

• Interlacement of circles is achieved by carving a design unit consisting of overlapping curved bands, and then printing it in four-step rotation.

• An interlaced effect is achieved by arranging rectangles in a lattice pattern.

• Interlaced design units in four-step rotation, using an adhesive foam printing block.

The effect of interlacement can also be achieved by the arrangement of the units. A rectangular shape stamped alternately in vertical and horizontal positions will look like a woven lattice, as shown in the illustration. Shading with partial overprints can accentuate the illusion.

Grouping

Small design units grouped to form larger shapes can then be treated as single units and repeated in any of the standard arrangements. Small design units can also be repeated to form lines, with the lines forming networks of various kinds, as illustrated. In another method of grouping units, a picture is formed by the outline of the printed area, as illustrated here in the picture of three buildings on page 22.

• Small design units grouped in clusters and in network lines.

• Design units grouped to form a picture of
three towers.

22

Controlling value

In most designs the stamp is inked for each print in order to make the prints uniformly dark. By printing twice before reinking, you can develop a dark-light alternation within the pattern, as shown in the illustration. When you need only light prints, ink the stamp for each print, but stamp it first on a piece of scrap paper to remove some of the ink. Try using these light prints as a background on which to stamp darker prints. The illustrations show two examples of this technique.

To give a single print a shaded look, you can reprint it with the stamp held at an angle to darken only one side of the first print, as shown. The shading will be

• Overprinted star design. The background of rotated diamond shapes was kept light in tone by first stamping the inked eraser on scrap paper to remove some of the ink. Overprints were then added with a fully inked triangular stamp from which narrow strips had been carved.

• Dark/light alteration of prints achieved by inking the stamp for every other print only.

• Light-toned square prints overprinted with two carved triangular stamps in rotation.

23

more pronounced if a second color is used for the partial print. You can achieve the same look by inking the stamp, printing it at an angle on scrap paper to remove most of the ink on one side, and then printing the half-inked stamp on the design.

• A trellis pattern printed with a rectangular stamp from which a shallow narrow line has been carved. Light prints were made first by stamping the entire stamp on scrap paper before printing. Tilting the eraser stamp to reprint the ends of each rectangular shape gives the pattern a shaded look.

Stenciling

Use stenciling in pattern design by masking out part of the area to be printed. The illustrations show two possible effects. Either the background or the image itself can be masked out with a cut-paper shape held in place with a bit of rubber cement. Rub off the cement when printing has been completed and stencil removed.

To make a printed image show up against a printed background, start by stamping the image on scrap paper as many times as it is to appear in the design. Cut each print out, leaving a narrow margin around the edge. Use a bit of rubber cement to fasten the prints in place on the paper that is to be printed. Print over the entire area using a different stamp, remove the paper shapes, and rub off the rubber cement. Then print the first image in each of the empty spaces left by the stencils.

• A paper stencil masked all but the printed area in this design. The Christmas ornament shape was cut from a sheet of scrap paper and discarded, and the remaining stencil was taped over a clean sheet of paper. The entire sheet was then printed with rows of various small shapes. The loop and cord were added with felt marker.

• A paper stencil masked only the area where the printed image was to appear against the printed background. A butterfly image printed on scrap paper was outlined, cut out, and rubber-cemented to a fresh sheet of paper. The entire sheet was printed with the background geometric pattern. The butterfly stencil was then removed, and the butterfly image was printed in the slightly larger white space.

CHAPTER TWO

Basic supplies

The only equipment needed for stamp pad printing is an inked stamp pad, a stamp, and a piece of paper. The additional materials listed here have uses mentioned in this book and are included to broaden your printing experience.

Stamp pads

Stamp pads are usually available in several colors, in two sizes, and in foam and in felt. The felt pads seem to coat the stamps more evenly. I also recommend a large pad when you need to ink a large design unit, although some large units can be inked by patting back and forth over a small stamp pad. Note that it is difficult to ink soft plastic blocks this way without making creases in the block where it touches the metal edge of the stamp pad box. Your best bet then is to use the large pads.

Inks

Stamp pad inks are available in several colors—red, black, purple, blue, green, brown, and orange. If you must have another color in parts of your pattern, try inking your stamp by coloring it with a felt marker. Be generous with your use of ink, reinking the pad frequently to ensure good prints. Since stamp pad inks may fade, printer's inks or acrylic paints are used in some of the projects that follow.

Paper

Newsprint in large rolls is sold for a very reasonable price at newspaper offices. Install one of these rolls on a horizontal rod near your worktable. Mimeograph paper is also inexpensive and comes in assorted pastel colors. Typing paper, except for the erasable kind, which you should not use, takes a good print. It is also lightweight enough to enable you to see the lines when working over a sheet of graph paper or other network guide.

Graph paper of various kinds is not only helpful as a guide to correct placement of prints in a final printing of a design, but it will also suggest arrangements of prints more complex than you could visualize without its guidelines. To get a perfect shape when cutting a diamond or square stamp, make sample prints on

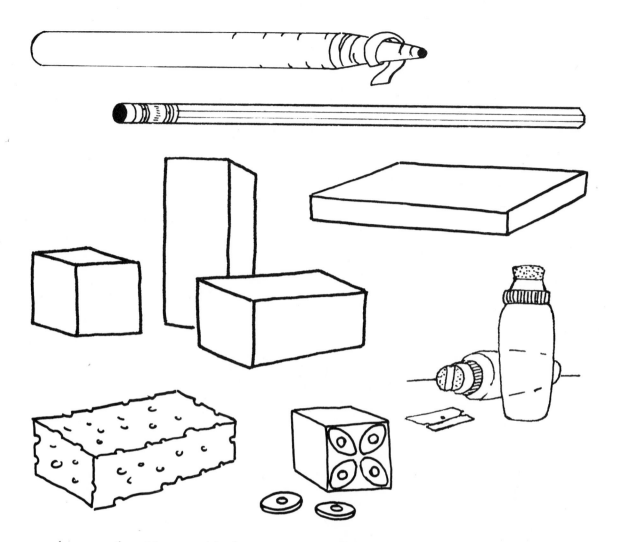

graph paper, then trim any side that overlaps the guidelines.

Stamps

Stamps can be made from any number of easily accessible items. Erasers of various kinds, soft plastic modeling compound (the nonhardening clay used in kindergartens), and many household items make excellent stamps. Squares of adhesive foam and felt, sold with footcare products at pharmacies, can be cut into shapes and affixed to blocks of wood or pieces of cardboard for use as printing blocks.

• **Common stationery and household items make excellent stamps. Shown here are a typewriter eraser, a pencil eraser, gum erasers, a vinyl eraser, sponge-topped stamp-moistening jars, a large sponge, and corn pads.**

Some small sponges make good prints, although each image may have to be stamped twice to get it dark enough. Large sponges, carved and inked with acrylic or latex paint, can duplicate almost any eraser print pattern on a grand scale.

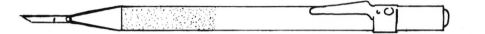

• An artist's (X-acto) knife is a useful tool for carving curved or intricate designs.

Cutting tools

A single-edged razor blade is the best tool for making straight cuts in eraser and sponge stamps. Curved or intricate cuts are more easily made with the pointed blade of an artist's (X-acto) knife. Keep a supply of fresh blades on hand, as they dull quickly, especially when they have been used to carve sponges. Use ordinary household scissors to cut adhesive foam and felt pieces.

Light table

A light table (the full-size or portable type used by graphic designers) makes graph paper guidelines visible even through a heavy drawing paper. If you have no light table and do not want to go through a lot of expense or trouble, tape a sheet of graph paper to a window with good lighting, tape typing paper over it, then print. The working position is awkward, so it is only practical for printing the final version of a previously developed pattern.

You may also be able to improvise a light table from discards or materials on hand. An old shower door, for example, laid across two small shelf units at table height will provide you with plenty of elbow room. If the door panel is made of rippled glass, lay a sheet of window glass over it for a smooth work surface. Window glass alone is not strong enough to serve as a light table. A lamp set on the floor under the glass panel will provide the light source needed when duplicating a design or using graph paper guidelines for the correct placement of prints.

Printing blocks

Printing blocks are needed as backing for lightweight printing materials such as adhesive foam. A child's wooden blocks, jar tops, and cardboard squares all can be used as printing blocks. Cardboard is acceptable, but it becomes dog-eared after it has been used for a while and the corners may smudge the design being printed. Cardboard is practical for small projects, though, if care is taken not to press down on the corners. Be sure to plan your design to fit the size of the printing block. Do not put a small design in the center of a large block's surface or you will not be able to place the prints accurately.

• Jar tops provide support and work well as printing blocks for lightweight stamps.

Miscellaneous items

A wide, transparent ruler with graph lines is a great help in pattern work. Keep a metal or metal-edged ruler on hand to be used when cutting straight lines with a sharp blade. For printing large areas you will probably need a yardstick.

Pencils, masking tape, white glue, and felt markers in different sizes and colors are useful items to have in a handy place.

Most stamp pad ink will not wash off of furniture or clothing, so children using it should wear smocks and work on a table covered with newspapers.

CHAPTER THREE

Typewriter eraser prints

A pencil-shaped typewriter eraser will print a small dot. The illustrations on the next few pages show just some of the pattern possibilities. The size of the dot, of course, depends on the size of the eraser. Since different companies make different sizes, it is to your advantage to have a wide variety of brands at your disposal. A typewriter eraser print is most useful as a detail in patterns formed by large shapes, but it can also be used as a very small repeat. The eraser is too small to be cut into anything but a very simple shape, but it is nevertheless worth some experimental carving.

A typewriter eraser is also a good tool for making corrections. Use it to fill in flaws in an otherwise perfectly printed design.

Keep typewriter erasers, as well as pencil erasers, in a mug, pointed end up, for easy visibility.

• Eraser stamps stored in a mug, carved side up for easy visibility.

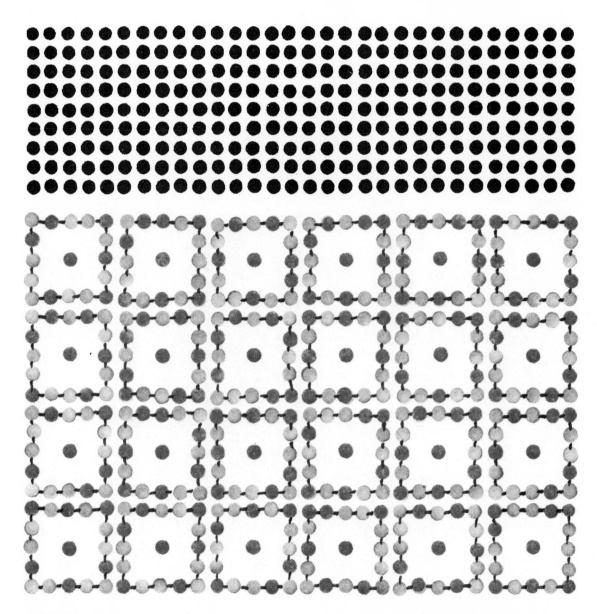

• A basic pattern made with typewriter eraser prints.

• Dark-light values of typewriter eraser prints done in a square network. Felt marker lines connect the dots.

- Felt marker lines connecting a square arrangement of typewriter eraser prints form octagons in alternate spaces.

- Erasers from two different manufacturers were used to create clusters of prints in two sizes. Felt marker lines form the stems within each cluster.

31

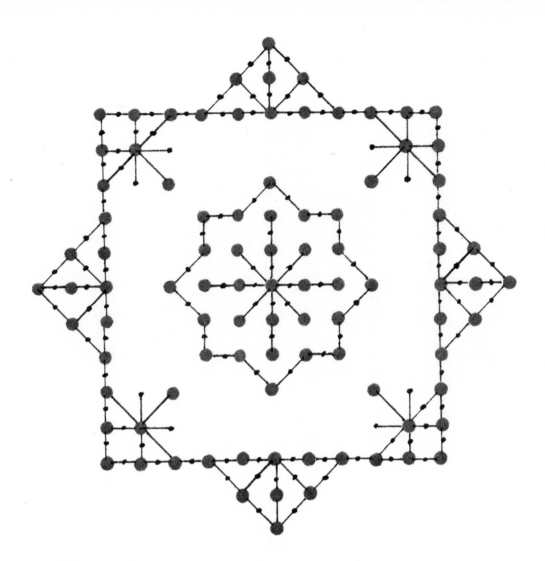

• Typewriter eraser prints in large overlapping squares become a star pattern when connected with fine marker lines.

• Two sizes of typewriter eraser prints in a
chevron pattern.

DOLLHOUSE WALLPAPER

Printing your own wallpaper for a doll-house will give you an incentive to design a series of patterns using very small design units. Test your ingenuity by using a type-writer eraser to print a sheet of polka dots, working over graph paper for accurate

• An all-over pattern of typewriter eraser dots given variety by the addition of prints made with a carved typewriter eraser.

spacing. Use a photocopying machine to make several duplicates of the pattern, then change the character of each by add-ing connecting lines or other prints.

• **Dollhouse wallpaper from a pattern of typewriter eraser prints.**

Materials
2 typewriter erasers, same size
stamp pads and inks, red and black
single-edged razor blade
masking tape
dark-lined graph paper
lightweight paper, cut to fit dollhouse wall
spray adhesive

Instructions
1. Use the single-edged razor blade to cut a thin strip from the center of the tip of one typewriter eraser.
2. With small pieces of masking tape fasten a sheet of graph paper to the work surface. Tape lightweight paper over it. Make sure dark lines of the graph paper show through.
3. Using the graph paper spaces as a guide to placement, print red dots over the entire sheet.
4. Use the cut-eraser tip to make black prints connecting the red dots in most of the vertical rows.
5. Vary the pattern by leaving some rows plain and by adding horizontally positioned black prints in others, using the wallpaper shown in the photograph as a guide.
6. Spray the back of the printed paper with adhesive. Fit it against the dollhouse wall, correcting placement before pressing it firmly in place.

CHAPTER FOUR

Pencil eraser prints

The unused eraser of a new pencil makes a clear, round print, and the pencil shank itself provides a comfortable handle that helps in accurate placement of the prints. Some variety stores carry large pencils with erasers, as well as pencils of the standard size. Jumbo pencils can be found in souvenir shops, and these have erasers that make ½-inch (1.27-cm) prints. Keep pencils of each size on hand. Cut some of the erasers and use some whole, leaving a few to be cut as new ideas occur to you. The illustrations on the next few pages will serve as examples of the kind of patterns that can be developed by using pencil eraser prints.

• A basic pencil eraser pattern worked over graph paper for correct spacing.

• A flower pattern suggested by groups of
four pencil eraser prints. A second eraser
was carved to make leaf-shaped prints, and
the stems and centers were drawn with a felt
marker.

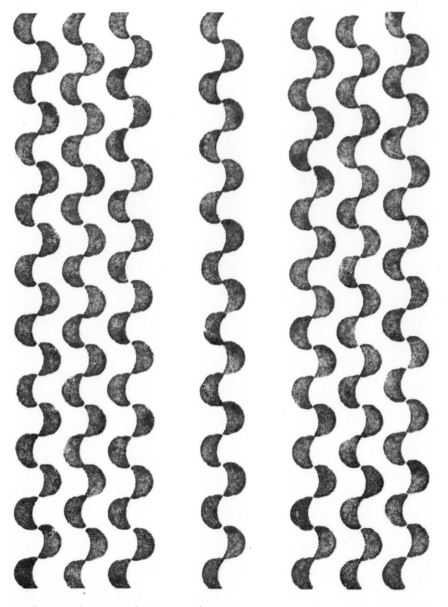

• A curved cut in a large pencil eraser, made with the empty eraser casing of a second pencil, was printed in rows to create this pattern.

• A bead pattern with overprint shading (see page 23). Felt marker lines connect the "beads."

• A pattern of pencil eraser prints worked over compass-drawn guidelines. Erasers in two sizes were given curved cuts with empty eraser casings, a third eraser was carved in a teardrop shape, and a fourth was used as a whole.

• In this pattern half-cut eraser prints suggest leaves, and curving marker lines create the branches.

• This rigid plant form is suggested by heavy felt marker stem lines and pencil eraser prints.

RECIPE COLLECTION

Design a printed border to decorate pages for your recipe collection. Cut out the center part of a sheet of blue-lined graph paper and print the remaining paper frame with a pencil eraser pattern. The decorative paper border is then used with each recipe sheet as it is run through a good photocopying machine. The light blue lines of the graph paper will not show up on the copies, but the printed border will. Duplicates of your completed recipe collection would be welcome gifts for faraway family members.

Materials
2 typewriter erasers, same size
jumbo pencil with eraser
stamp pad and ink, black
single-edged razor blade
scissors

• **Scalloped border made of half-cut pencil and typewriter eraser prints with felt marker detailing.**

• **Recipe collection pages decorated with eraser print borders.**

graph paper with light blue lines, 5
     squares to the inch
masking tape
ruler
fine-line felt marker, black
blank sheets of typing paper
photocopying machine
paper punch
looseleaf binder

Instructions

1. Use the single-edged razor blade to cut off half of the tip of one typewriter eraser and half of the pencil eraser.
2. Cut a 5¾- by 7¾-inch (14.6- by 19.7-cm) rectangle from the center of a sheet of graph paper. Tape the remaining paper frame to the work surface.
3. Outline the inner border of the paper frame, ¼ inch (6.35 mm) from the cut edge, using a ruler and a fine-line felt marker.
4. Print a scallop along the outline with the half-cut typewriter eraser, following the design in the illustration as a guide or creating a design of your own. Each print should be centered over one small space in the graph paper.
5. Add a second outline around the border prints, ¼ inch out from the first. Then print around that with the half-cut pencil eraser, forming a second and larger scallop. Each of these larger scallops will cover two spaces of the graph paper.
6. Fill in the spaces between the pencil-eraser scallops with typewriter eraser prints. Add felt marker dots and stem lines.
7. Make photocopies of your recipes, centering one recipe sheet on the printed frame, with both the recipe and frame facedown on the photocopying machine. Leave the frame in place as each recipe is copied and removed.
8. Punch holes in the photocopied pages and assemble them in a looseleaf binder.

STATIONERY

It is not difficult to hand-print identical designs on lightweight sheets of stationery. Once a satisfactory design has been worked out, position and print it carefully on one piece of stationery. Reproduce the design quickly and accurately by laying each of the other sheets over the master copy and using it as a guide.

Experiment with plant motifs by drawing sets of branching stems, then printing the ends of the branches with a variety of stamps. You might find that a stamp you had carved for another pattern will be more interesting as a leaf than one you originally planned for that use. Use a small simplified version of the motif to decorate the edges of the box, if you wish.

Materials
pencil with eraser
stamp pad and ink, any color
single-edged razor blade
ruler
fine-line felt marker
stationery
stationery box
wide-line felt marker
white glue

Instructions

1. Use the single-edged razor blade to cut a wedge from the pencil eraser.
2. With the pencil, starting ¾ inch (1.905 cm) from the top of the page, draw a vertical stem 1½ inches (3.81 cm) long in the top center portion of one sheet of stationery.
3. Draw three smaller stems, slanting upward, on each side of the vertical stem. Add an eraser print at the end of each stem. Position the eraser so that the stem's tip touches the point of the notch.

• **Carved eraser prints and felt pen lines created this plant form motif.**

4. Use the printed sheet as the master copy, laying subsequent sheets over it to retrace the position of the stem and branch lines with a fine-line felt marker before stamping the print.

5. Following illustration, use the cut pencil eraser to stamp seven prints.

6. Cut four strips of paper ½ inch (1.27 cm) longer than the four sides of the box, with enough allowance to fold over the top edge and down the inside of the box.

7. Use a ruler and wide-line felt marker to draw a line along one edge of each strip of paper. Draw a lightly penciled line ¼ inch (6.35 mm) above it. Use the fine-line felt marker to draw ¼-inch-long stems ⅜ inch (9.525 mm)

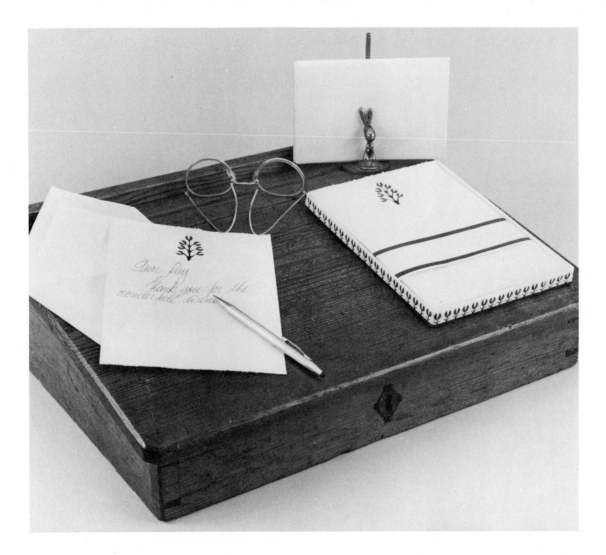

- **Eraser-printed stationery and decorated box.**

apart along the black borderline. Use the penciled line as a starting point for each stem, erasing it when finished. Add two short branch lines to each.

Print the wedge-cut pencil eraser at the top of each stem line.

8. Spread a very light coat of white glue on the back of each strip of paper. Press it against one side of the box, folding the top over and into the box and overlapping the corners slightly. Smooth and press the paper firmly into place.

CERAMIC TILES

Inexpensive unglazed tiles are available for purchase at ceramic studios in most communities. The tiles, called *greenware,* can be decorated with colored underglaze (available at the ceramic studio), fired by the studio, then coated with clear over- glaze and refired. Designs can be printed on the tiles with pencil erasers or small sponges. Keep in mind that tiles at the greenware stage must be handled very carefully because they are extremely frag- ile.

The instructions here are for small matching tiles. For larger tiles, add an ex- tra border such as the one shown.

• **Pencil eraser prints in two sizes, with typewriter eraser prints and felt marker con-** **necting lines worked within multiple borders.**

• **These ceramic tiles were underglazed with eraser prints, fired, and then overglazed and fired again.**

Materials
pencil with eraser
jumbo pencil with eraser
typewriter eraser
greenware tile, 3¼ inches (8.255 cm)
    square
jar of translucent liquid underglaze, blue
water, small amount
aluminum foil
very small watercolor paintbrush
overglaze, clear
wide, flat watercolor paintbrush

Instructions
1. Use a pencil to draw guidelines on the tile for the design illustrated or use a design of your own. (Pencil lines will burn out when the tile is fired.) Mark the exact center of the tile with a pencil (to find the center, draw crossing diagonal lines from corner to corner), and draw a border line ⅛ inch (3.175 mm) from the edge all around.
2. Dilute a small amount of underglaze to a milklike consistency with some water and mix them together on a piece of aluminum foil. Ink the standard-size pencil eraser in the diluted underglaze, then print it in the exact center of the tile, using a light touch. Print four large dots around it, using the eraser of the jumbo pencil.
3. With the typewriter eraser, print the spaces between the large dots. Then print a border of typewriter eraser dots ⅛ inch (3.175 mm) in from the edge of the tile, along your penciled guideline. Print the corner motifs with one pencil eraser print in each corner and five typewriter eraser prints curved over it.
4. Use a very small watercolor brush and the diluted underglaze to paint all stem lines. Paint connecting lines between the dots forming the border, and with the tip of the brush, add very small dots around the central and corner clusters of prints.
5. Return the tile to the ceramic studio to be fired.
6. Thin the overglaze with water in a small bowl. (Follow manufacturer's directions.) Use the wide brush to coat the tile with the glaze with thick, flowing strokes. Do not go back over the painted areas to smooth what may look like an uneven coverage. Let dry, then recoat the tile with undiluted glaze.
7. Return the tile to the ceramic studio for the final firing.

CHAPTER FIVE

Gum eraser prints

The illustrations on the next few pages feature just some of the kinds of patterns you can print with a gum eraser (also called "artgum"). The ends of rectangular gum erasers can be used to make square prints or the sides can be printed as rectangles. The corner edges will print straight lines. The erasers can be used whole or cut into many smaller shapes. Gum is soft enough to carve easily, so you can cut fairly intricate designs in its surface. Designs should be carved only on the uncut sides of these pieces. Because the cut sides are slightly uneven, they will not give a clear print.

Since gum is so soft, some improvised tools may be used to cut it. An easy way to cut round holes in the gum is to remove a pencil eraser from its metal casing and use the edge of the casing to cut the holes. Press the casing into the eraser, then tilt the pencil slightly to pull out and remove the circular piece. Squeeze the

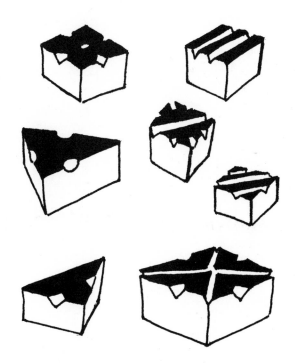

• Gum erasers carved in a number of ways.

49

• **Remove a pencil eraser from its casing with pliers and use the empty casing as a cutting tool.**

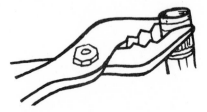

• **Pinch a pencil eraser's empty casing with pliers for an oval- or teardrop-shaped cutting tool.**

casing with a pair of pliers to make a teardrop or oval shape. The lip of an empty small tin can will make curved cuts, and aspic cutters or tiny cookie cutters are also useful. Fine copper tubing (from the hardware store) comes in a variety of shapes and is helpful for cutting out small areas from gum design. Also useful is a single-edged razor blade clipped with a wire cutter into very small chisel-like tools. Shield the upper edge with masking tape.

Draw intricate shapes that might be difficult to cut freehand with felt marker on the gum before cutting. You can also draw them on paper, lay the penciled drawing facedown on the artgum, and then burnish the back side of the paper with the rounded part of a spoon. The outline will be transferred to the eraser surface.

• **A gum eraser pattern.**

- Star-shaped spaces are created when prints are made with a square gum eraser that has been notched on all four sides.

- A printed pattern made with the same stamp used in the illustration on top. Narrow lines cut from the eraser surface leave weblike spaces against a dark background.

51

• Light-toned triangular prints with smaller
dark overprints (see page 23). The arrangement includes areas of both two- and four-
step rotation.

• Cuts made with an eraser casing pinched flat on one side with a pair of pliers. Pattern shows use of both two- and three-step rotation and a secondary cross-shaped pattern formed by the lighter prints.

• Wave pattern made with a gum stamp in which curved cuts were made with the fine point of an artist's (X-acto) knife.

SHELF LINER

Hand-print a shelf liner like the one shown here or in any pattern you want, and, if you wish, line your kitchen drawers with an all-over pattern of the same print. The addition of felt marker lines makes color possibilities unlimited.

• Cross-band design carved in a square gum eraser, then printed in rows between wide felt marker lines.

• Shelf liner printed with a cross-band pattern, then bordered with wide felt marker lines.

Materials

gum eraser
stamp pad and ink, blue
single-edged razor blade
unglazed shelf paper, white
scissors
pencil
yardstick
pinking shears
indelible wide-line felt marker, dark blue
indelible fine-line felt marker, light green,
     light purple, or any three colors of
     your choice
double-sided adhesive tape

Instructions

1. Use a fine-line felt marker to draw the
   cross-band design in the illustration
   (see illustrations) on your gum eraser,
   or create a design of your own. Using
   the razor blade, carve away the un-
   marked areas of the gum eraser surface.
2. Measure your shelf and cut a sheet of
   unglazed shelf paper to fit it, leaving a
   1½-inch (3.81-cm) allowance to be
   folded down over the front edge of the
   shelf.
3. Use the pencil and yardstick to draw a
   light line ¼ inch (6.35 mm) in from the
   outside edge of the shelf paper. Cut
   along this line with pinking shears.
4. Draw a dark blue marker line ¼ inch
   (6.35 mm) in from and parallel to the
   pinked edge.
5. With the carved gum, print along the
   blue line.
6. Draw another wide blue line along the
   upper edge of the prints.

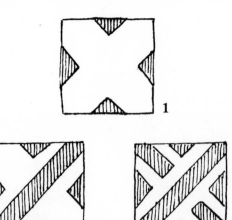

• To carve a cross-band design: (1) cut a
small triangular piece from each of the
sides, with the tip of each triangle aligned
over the midpoint of each side; (2) cut a diagonal strip from the lower left corner to the
upper right corner, leaving uncut portions
between the strip and the triangles; and (3)
cut two short strips, one from the lower
right and one from the upper left corners,
leaving uncut areas between these strips and
the triangles and between these strips and
the central diagonal strip.

7. Color the center diamond-shaped
   spaces with a light purple felt marker.
   Color the small triangles light green.
8. Install the paper on your shelf, folding
   the printed border down over the front
   edge. Put a small piece of double-sided
   tape under each corner to help keep
   the liner in place.

GIFT WRAP

Brown kraft paper takes a good print, is a warm and attractive background color, and is the right weight for wrapping packages. Printed strips of the paper can be used as matching ribbon for the packages. Use double-sided tape to attach bows from graduated loops of the paper ribbon. Print an assortment of coordinated patterns by using the same stamps and colors in several arrangements. The package on the left on page 59 features the design shown in the illustration. The other package designs in the photograph are variations of that design.

Materials
2 gum erasers
typewriter eraser
pencil with eraser
stamp pad and inks, red and black
single-edged razor blade
scissors
brown kraft paper
wide-line felt marker, red
yardstick or *T* square
fine-line felt marker, black
double-sided adhesive tape

Instructions
1. Carve the two gum erasers in the shapes illustrated, a four-petal flower and a smaller triangular shape, or create a design of your own.
2. Cut a sheet of brown paper large enough to cover the box you intend to wrap.
3. With the red felt marker, draw parallel lines across the paper at 2-inch (5.08-cm) intervals. Use a yardstick or *T* square to keep the lines straight. Draw a red line along the center of alternate stripes.
4. Print flower shapes in red along the centers of the wide stripes. A ruled pencil line will help keep the prints straight. Flower-shaped prints should be ½ inch (1.27 cm) apart.
5. Use the pencil eraser to print black dots in the centers of the flower-shaped prints and in each of the spaces between them. With the black fine-line felt marker, draw short lines connecting the flowers and dots.
6. Stamp triangular prints ¼ inch (6.35 mm) apart along the upper and lower edges of the central stripe in alternate rows. Ink the stamp alternately with red and black ink, cleaning it between prints by stamping on scrap paper.
7. Print a pencil eraser dot in red at the tip of each of the triangular prints. Use the typewriter eraser to print small dots in the spaces between the triangles.
8. Print a strip of paper long enough to wrap around the box and four loops of paper in graduated lengths to be taped to the center as a bow.

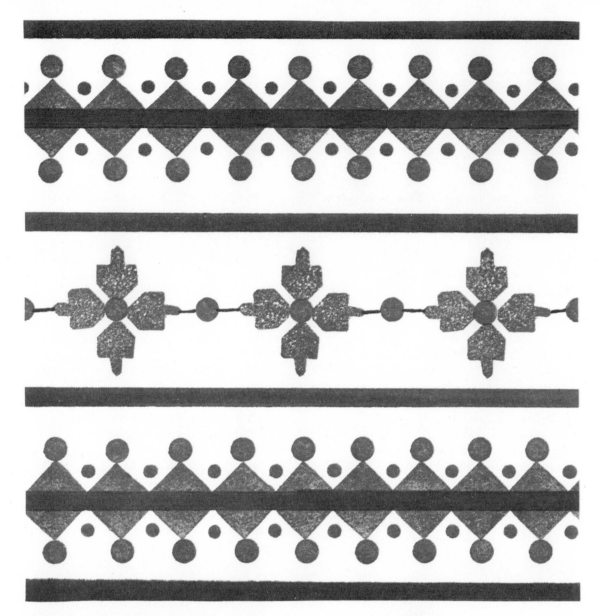

• Rows of pencil, typewriter, and carved gum eraser prints arranged between wide felt marker lines. Narrow strips were cut to divide a gum eraser surface into four small squares. The sides of each of the squares were then trimmed to give the shape in the prints.

• Gift packages wrapped in printed brown paper. The same gum eraser stamps and colored inks were used in different arrangements for coordinate patterns.

DECORATED EGGS

Even the shell of a hard-boiled egg makes a good printing surface. Just make sure that the egg is at room temperature as drops of moisture form on chilled eggs taken from the refrigerator, blurring the prints and making the eggs slippery. When printing several eggs, rest each of them in a crumpled paper towel to keep it from rolling. Then print the visible side of each egg. When the ink has dried, turn the eggs over and finish printing them.

The following instructions are for the egg in the foreground of the illustration.

Materials
gum eraser
stamp pads and inks, blue and black
single-edged razor blade
hard-boiled egg
pencil

Instructions
1. Carve a shallow, narrow strip from the surface of a small triangular piece of gum eraser. Use the design illustrated or create a design of your own.
2. Draw lightly penciled lines around the egg to help keep the rows of prints straight.
3. Print along the guidelines, beginning with a double row of blue prints in the center and working out from it, turning the triangular stamp in different directions for each of the rows. Follow the color scheme in the photograph or devise your own. Take care not to handle the egg more than necessary, or you might smear the fresh prints. If necessary, you can paint over small errors with typewriter correction fluid.

• Eggs printed with different stamps made from small pieces of gum eraser cut into triangular shapes.

- A pattern of stripes printed with a small triangular piece of eraser. The shallow, narrow line was cut from the eraser surface with a very sharp single-edged razor blade. The stamp was then turned in different directions to vary the patterns in the rows of prints.

PRINTED WALL, GEOMETRIC PATTERN

A wall printed in acrylic paint is completely washable, so it is practical for kitchen and bathroom areas. Since covering even a small wall with gum eraser prints is a project that requires patience, larger areas are better saved for sponged patterns. (See Chapter 8.) Print only on a wall that has been painted with flat washable latex paint. Glossy paint has a slippery surface that does not take a good print.

Nearly any kind of pattern can be printed on a wall in nearly any colors, so use your imagination!

Materials
gum eraser
acrylic paints, red, brown, and white
single-edged razor blade
yardstick
pencil
foil-covered baking sheet or tray
water, small amount
flat paintbrush, medium size
chair or ladder
paper towels
wet scrub cloth

Instructions
1. Carve the square surface of a gum eraser in a corner design such as the one illustrated or create a design of your own. Cut a small square piece from one corner of the eraser, then cut narrow strips forming two right angles, one nesting within the other. Use the corner of the single-edged blade to notch the inner edge of the larger remaining strip. The design consists of four prints in rotation forming a square.
2. Use the yardstick and pencil to make light guidelines on the area of the wall to be printed. You will not need a penciled line for every row of prints, but an occasional line will be a help.
3. Squeeze out small amounts of each color of acrylic paint on the foil-covered baking sheet. Mix colors—the wall in the room in the photograph was printed in red, tan (mixture of brown and white), pink (mixture of red and white), and a red-brown mixture. Dilute the colors on the baking sheet with a few drops of water and use a brush to spread each of the colors over a small area of the foil. The foil will act as a stamp pad. Set the baking sheet on a chair or ladder at a convenient height.
4. Ink the gum eraser stamp by pressing it several times over one of the acrylic paints on the baking sheet. Beginning at the top corner of the wall, make four prints of the same color, reinking and rotating the stamp a quarter turn for each print. Erase any misprints by washing immediately (acrylic paints dry very quickly) with a damp scrub cloth. Clean the eraser by stamping it on a paper towel. Print the next group of four in a different color and continue printing, changing colors at random. Plan spacing between four-print groups so that complete prints will fill the area with no half-spaces left at the margins. If this seems to be unavoidable, leave the partial spaces until the rest of the wall has been printed. Then cut off part of the eraser and print the remaining spaces with it.
5. Allow to dry, then wash off the penciled guidelines.

• Dressing room wall printed with a carved gum eraser and acrylic paints. The small area of prints appears larger because of the reflection in the adjoining mirror.

• A cornerlike design printed in four-step rotation. Strips forming nested right angles were carved from a square eraser, then notches were cut in the outer edge of the remaining middle section.

CHAPTER SIX

Vinyl eraser prints

Vinyl erasers, which usually come in white rectangular shapes, are very firm, have a smooth consistency, and make excellent prints. Because it is dense, vinyl is a little more difficult to carve than gum, but it does not have gum's tendency to crumble. Although the two materials are similar, you will find with experimentation that there is a different "feel" to the two kinds of stamps, and you will probably develop a preference for one or the other. The patterns on the next few pages give you some idea of the vinyl eraser's potential in pattern formation.

• A basic vinyl eraser pattern within a brick network.

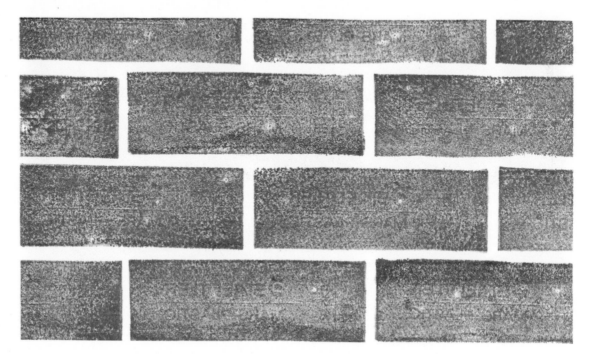

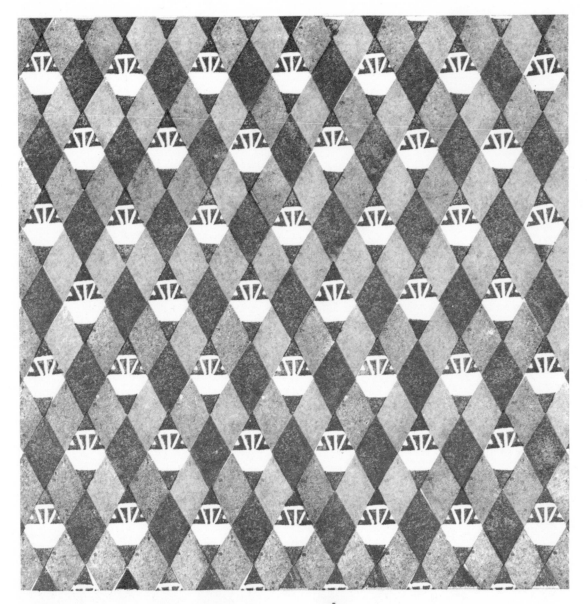

• Diamond-shaped stamps printed in two
tones as a diamond network, with two
smaller carved triangular stamps printed in
the spaces.

• A vinyl eraser, cut into an equilateral triangle, was carved with stripes in order to
print this pattern in a combination of two-
and four-step rotation.

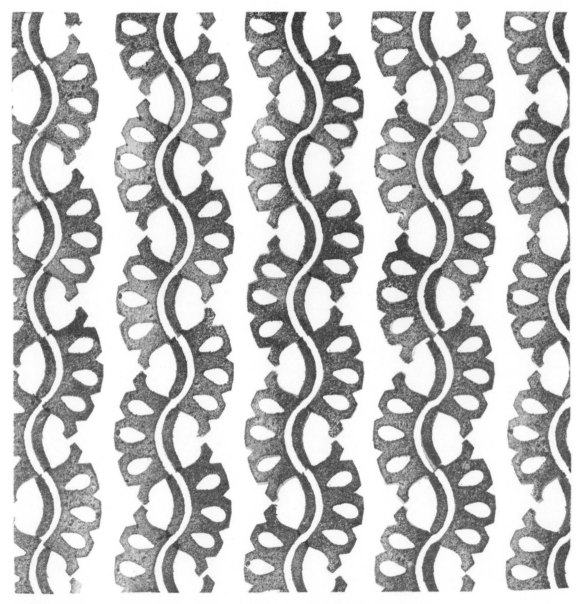

• Stripes printed with a vinyl eraser stamp carved in a quarter-circle design. Flame-shaped cuts are made with the end of a piece of brass tubing (from the hardware store). The rounded cuts were made with the pointed blade of an artist's (X-acto) knife, following lines printed on the eraser with bottle caps in three sizes.

• The same carved quarter-circle stamp used in the illustration opposite. Here it is printed in rotation for a pattern built out from a central point. Triangular gum and pencil eraser prints added.

• A traditional quilt block pattern of diamonds planned over triangular graph paper and printed in two values. Begin by printing a central arrangement of diamonds in rotation, then enlarge the pattern by working outward.

• "Baby Blocks," an example of a traditional quilt pattern worked within a hexagon network. Printed over triangular paper, an eraser cut in a diamond shape was inked just once for each group of three prints, giving three-dimensional shading to each hexagon in the pattern.

70

MAILING TAPE AND LABELS

Decorate gift packages for mailing by trimming them with printed brown tape. Parcel post tape, the kind that needs to be moistened for use, is one brown mailing tape that is unglazed and will take a good print. You can also make address labels from pieces of the tape or from squares of brown kraft paper, then border-print them with small stamps.

Materials

2 vinyl erasers
typewriter eraser
stamp pad and ink, any color
artist's knife with pointed blade (X-acto knife)
single-edged razor blade
ruler
scissors
brown mailing tape, parcel post type
package wrapped in white paper
fine-line felt marker, same color as stamp pad ink
white glue

• **A package wrapped and decorated in printed brown tape and labels.**

Instructions

1. If necessary, use a single-edged razor blade to cut one of the vinyl eraser's length to match the width of the brown tape. Use an artist's knife to carve it in the design illustrated or create a design of your own.
2. Measure the box and cut one piece of tape long enough to go around the four sides.
3. Ink one of the erasers by pressing it on a well-saturated stamp pad several times. Print along the entire length of the tape, holding the eraser stamp in a vertical position and reversing it for every second print. Make sure all spaces between prints are equal.
4. Print a typewriter eraser dot at the center of each of the flower-shaped spaces between pairs of prints.
5. Moisten the tape and wrap it tightly around the four sides of the box, keeping it centered between and parallel to the top and bottom edges of the box.
6. Cut mailing labels from the tape and border-print the edges with the small vinyl eraser, carved in a simple design. Glue the labels to the package.
7. Use the felt marker to draw a bow and string around the box.

• A vinyl eraser was carved in half of a motif. Then it was reversed for every other print to make a whole. A fine-pointed artist's (X-acto) knife is needed for carving narrow, curved strips such as these.

BOOK COVERS

Make durable book covers from hand-printed brown kraft paper. Give school-books and cookbooks protective covers in coordinated patterns or cover paperback books for distinctive but inexpensive gifts. You can, if you wish, make permanent covers by using a spray adhesive on the back of the paper. To give the book a finished look, add endpapers (using spray adhesive) in a smaller printed pattern.

Materials
2 vinyl erasers
stamp pad and ink, black
jumbo-sized pencil with eraser removed
    from its casing
single-edged razor blade
ruler
book to be covered
scissors
brown kraft paper
pencil
wide-line indelible felt marker, red
double-sided adhesive tape

Instructions
1. Carve the vinyl erasers in the designs illustrated or create designs of your own. Use the single-edged razor blade to cut a small triangular piece from two opposite sides of a square vinyl eraser and thin strips outlining the triangular cuts. Use the metal eraser casing on the jumbo pencil to cut half-circle pieces from the other two sides of the printing surface. On the smooth side of a ½-inch (1.27-cm) cube of vinyl eraser, carve a triangular shape from each of two opposite sides of the square surface. Carve strips which form a cross from corner to corner, but leave a small rectangular piece uncut in the center of the cross.

2. Measure the book that is to be covered. Cut a sheet of paper large enough to cover it, with a 2-inch (5.08-cm) allowance on each end.

3. Use the red felt marker with a ruler to draw a wide line along the lower margin of the paper. Print with the large eraser stamp along the upper edge of the line. Draw another red line above the prints, and print along the upper edge of it with the smaller eraser stamp. Continue printing rows of the two designs alternately, separating them with red felt marker stripes, until the paper is completely printed. Leave the center section of one row unprinted if you would like space to write in the book's title.

4. Wrap the printed paper around the book, folding the two ends inside the front and back covers. Hold the printed cover in place with small pieces of double-sided adhesive tape under each corner.

• A pattern formed with two gum erasers printed in rows between felt marker stripes. Half-circle shapes in the larger eraser were cut with the metal eraser casing from a jumbo souvenir pencil.

• Book covers printed on heavy brown kraft
paper. The same prints are arranged differently for coordinate patterns.

REUSABLE GIFT BOX

Some hand-printed designs are too attractive to be crumpled and discarded after use as gift wrap. When this is the case, cover a gift box in such a way that it can be reused. A box with a lid that slides completely down over the sides is the best kind, as the lid can be covered with the gift wrap, while the bottom of the box can be left uncovered. Adjust the design to fit the top and side panels and use spray adhesive to fix the decorated paper perma-

• **Central prints in four-step rotation, with pairs of prints in two-step rotation at each side. The pattern is made with two carved vinyl eraser stamps, then enclosed in wide bands of felt marker color.**

nently to the box lid. It can then be kept by the recipient for use as decorative storage for small items.

The box shown in the illustration is decorated with a stamp designed to work in rotation. The stamp, carved in a diagonal design, was used to make a group of four prints around the center point of the box top. A pair of prints in two-step rotation was added at each side of the center group. The sides of the box were decorated with the same units, arranged differently. Wide felt marker lines enclose the printed areas.

• **Decorated gift box. Paper is printed with a vinyl eraser. The back is then sprayed with adhesive to make a reusable lid for a sturdy box.**

Materials

2 vinyl erasers
stamp pad and ink, black
single-edged razor blade
ruler
cardboard box, approximately 6½ inches
    square, 3½ inches deep (16.5 cm
    square, 8.9 cm deep)
unglazed shelf paper, white
scissors
graph paper
masking tape
indelible felt markers, beige, gray, black
spray adhesive

Instructions

1. Carve the vinyl erasers in the designs illustrated or create some of your own.
Cut two parallel diagonal strips from the
surface of a 1-inch (2.54-cm) square of
vinyl eraser. Cut three triangular pieces
from one corner and two from the opposite corner, using the illustration as a
guide. Cut a second vinyl eraser on a
½-inch (1.27-cm) cube and carve the
smooth surface in a cross-band design.
Cut a narrow, shallow strip from one
corner to its opposite corner, and a
shorter strip leading from each of the
other two corners toward the center of
the printing surface. Each of these two
short strips should stop just short of
joining the opposing diagonal cut.

2. Measure the box lid and cut a sheet of
shelf paper to fit it, adding an allowance of several inches to fold inside the
edge.

3. Set the box lid upside down on a piece
of graph paper. Center it and trace
around it. Turn the lid on its side and
position it so that one side rests against
a side of the traced square. Trace that
section. Repeat with each side, so that
the final drawing resembles a box with
all of its sides laid out flat.

4. Fasten the graph paper to the work
surface with small pieces of masking
tape.

5. Cut out the shelf paper along your
traced outline. Center the sheet of shelf
paper over the taped graph paper and
tape it down.

6. Using the graph paper lines as a guide
for placement, print the design on the
shelf paper. Add border stripes and
color parts of the design with indelible
felt markers.

7. Center the design on the top of the gift
box, fold the side sections down, and
miter the corners with sharp creases.
Remove the paper, spray the back with
adhesive, and cover the box, folding
the excess under at the bottom edge of
the lid.

PRINTED WALL, FLORAL PATTERN

The basic ingredients of a floral pattern are stems, leaves, and flowers. The stems can be long and sweep upward, droop downward at the ends, or jut along at abrupt angles. Flower shapes can be varied in size and shape, arranged singly or in clusters. They can be seen full-faced or in profile and might be accompanied by buds. Study fabric designs and china patterns to see how others have used flowers and leaves as pattern elements. You will find that several kinds of flowers and leaves are often shown growing from the same stem, that tendrils, thorns, and berries are added with more concern for design than botanical accuracy. Bumble bees, butterflies, and birds are favorite extras used to add interest to some of the larger spaces between branches.

Begin your floral wall pattern by painting a few swerving stem lines at intervals across the wall. Then add flowers, berries, and leaves with eraser prints in acrylic and latex paints. Your pattern will evolve slowly and will most easily be done in stages spread over several days. You will need time to study the developing pattern in order to judge where additional prints should be made.

Materials
3 vinyl erasers
1 pencil with eraser
jumbo pencil with eraser
typewriter eraser
flat latex paint for base coat, antique white
½ pint flat latex paint for prints, antique white
acrylic paints, red, brown, and yellow
single-edged razor blade
masking tape
colored chalk, dark enough to show up on wall

foil-covered baking sheet or tray
water, small amount
small watercolor paintbrush, pointed
scrub cloth
soapy water
flat paintbrush, approximately 2 inches (5 cm) wide

Instructions
1. Carve the vinyl erasers using the designs illustrated as a guide or use some designs of your own. You will need one long triangle-shaped stamp and three leaf-shaped stamps of different sizes, as well as the pencil and typewriter erasers. Cut one of the vinyl erasers into a triangular shape 2¼ inches (5.7 cm) long and 1 inch (2.54 cm) wide at its base. Cut a large notch in the base and carve three narrow shallow strips across the central area of the stamp's printing surface. Carve the three leaf-shaped stamps, making the largest approximately 2 inches (5.08 cm) long, and ½ inch (1.27 cm) wide across the center. Cut a flame-shaped section from the center of the large leaf-shaped stamp.

2. Protect adjoining walls, ceiling, and baseboard with strips of masking tape. Paint the wall with a washable flat latex in antique white. Allow to dry thoroughly.

3. Use a piece of colored chalk to draw several wavy lines from floor to ceiling on the wall. The lines should divide the wall into nearly equal sections.

4. Add a few long, sweeping branch lines to each main stem, standing at a distance to see whether the branches are evenly distributed over the wall area.

5. When the composition satisfies you, mix some of the latex with brown acrylic on the foil-covered baking sheet. Keep the color fairly light. Add a few drops of water to the paint, so that it is

- Plant forms printed with a carved triangle, leaf shapes, and typewriter eraser dots.

• **A wall printed in a floral pattern in acrylic and latex paints. The plant forms in the illustration on page 80 were enlarged for use on this wall.**

the consistency of light cream. With the pointed watercolor brush, paint along the chalk-drawn stems and branches, working from the ceiling downward and from left to right to avoid smears. Slide the side of your hand along the wall for long, smooth strokes. Wash any mistakes off immediately, using a scrub cloth and soapy water.

6. Mix red acrylic paint with some water on the foil-covered baking sheet. Use the flat brush to spread the paint over several inches of the foil. Ink the trian-

gular vinyl eraser by stamping it on the red paint area of the foil. Use it to print flower shapes at the ends of some of the branch lines on the wall. Reink the stamp for each print.

7. With the three leaf-shaped vinyl erasers, print leaves in the same way, using a mixture of yellow acrylic, latex, and water. Add smaller stems where needed.

8. Print red buds using the jumbo pencil eraser and print berries with a stand-ard-sized pencil eraser. Add light brown background dots with a typewriter eraser. Encircle some of them with red dots, using the same typewriter eraser.

9. Wash off any chalk lines that show. Use a small brush with antique white latex to correct any rough edges.

CHAPTER SEVEN

Adhesive foam and felt prints

Adhesive foam, sold in pharmacies with footcare products, is an ideal printing material. It is available in small sheets, which can be cut with scissors and then mounted on a printing block of cardboard or wood. The point of a compass or a large pin might be needed to catch the center of the protective backing in order to pull it loose to be removed.

Adhesive felt and corn and bunion pads of various shapes can also be used on printing blocks. The felt absorbs ink slowly, so it must be pressed repeatedly on a well-saturated stamp pad before it will make a good print. Pieces of foam and felt combined on the same block will give a two-toned print because of the difference in the absorbency of the materials.

Neoprene, a material used in ski clothes and wet suits for divers, is similar to the foam in the footcare products. Discarded neoprene garments or pieces sold as patches can be cut up and glued to a printing block. The material gives a print with a finely veined texture similar to that of leather.

A toothpick dipped in white glue can be used to draw lines or dots on the foam, felt, or neoprene pieces. When dry, the glue will print as detailing.

• A basic pattern printed with an adhesive foam callus pad mounted on a wooden block.

• A printing block made with four corn pads was used to make this pattern. Eraser prints and felt marker lines are added accents.

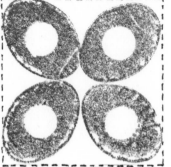

• Adhesive foam pieces glued to a child's building block and printed in four-step rotation.

• Shapes cut from adhesive felt, then glued to a child's building block, created this flower motif pattern.

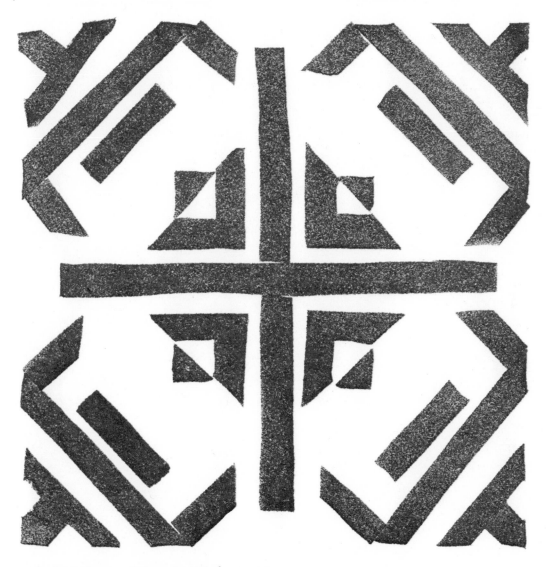

• A single large print made with foam strips glued onto a 6-inch (15.24-cm) block.

• Shapes of cut neoprene glued to a printing block, then printed over a square network on the diagonal.

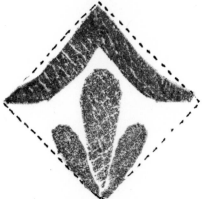

CARDBOARD CANNISTERS

Cover large cardboard cannisters, available at ice cream stores, with printed brown paper for use as wastebaskets, containers for dried flower arrangements, or just about anything. Smaller cartons, such as cut-down oatmeal containers, can also be decorated for other uses.

Materials

adhesive foam, ½ inch (1.27 cm) square
adhesive felt, 1¾ inches (4.4 cm) square
    and ¾ inches (1.9 cm) square
wooden block 2 inches (5.08 cm) square
wooden block 1 inch (2.54 cm) square
stamp pads and inks, red and brown
scissors
compass or large safety pin
cardboard carton, any size
brown kraft paper, large enough to cover
    carton
spray paint, tan
spray adhesive
white glue

Instructions

1. Cut the foam and felt into pieces, using the illustration as a guide or using a design of your own. For the pattern shown in the photograph, remove the protective backing from the ½-inch-square (1.27-cm-square)
piece of foam, center it on the larger of the two wooden blocks and press it in place.

    Cut the 1¾-inch (4.4-cm) square of felt into quarters diagonally. Cut the inner point off each of the resulting triangles, remove the protective backing and reassemble them in a framelike square along the edges of the large wooden block. Spread the four pieces slightly apart to let the diagonal cuts show. Then press them in place.

    Cut the ¾-inch (1.9-cm) piece of felt into quarters diagonally. Cut the inner point off each of the resulting triangles, remove the protective backing, and reassemble them as in step 2 on the small wooden block. Spread the pieces slightly apart as you did in step 2 and press them into place.

2. Measure and cut a piece of brown kraft paper large enough to cover the outside of the carton.

3. Spray-paint the inside of the carton, using two coats if needed for good coverage. Make sure the rim is covered as well.

4. Use a pencil and ruler to mark the paper in a grid of 2-inch (5.08-cm) squares. Keep the penciled lines light.

5. Ink the large printing block on the red stamp pad. Then print in each of the spaces of the penciled grid. Ink the small printing block on the brown stamp pad and stamp it over each of the red prints. Hold the felt block in place on the paper for a moment to get a good print. When the ink is dry, erase the penciled guidelines.

6. Spray the outside of the carton and the back of the printed paper with adhesive. Fit the paper around the carton, smoothing away wrinkles or air pockets with your hands. Seal the seam by placing a little bit of white glue on the back of the printed paper's edge.

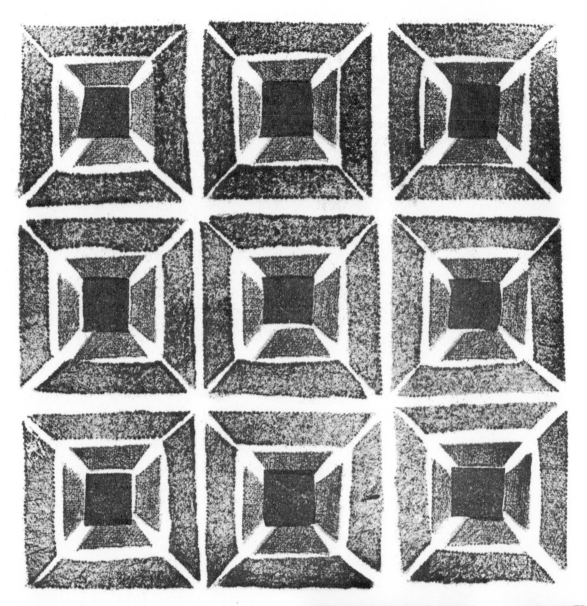

• Pattern made with two blocks. The larger block has a framelike design in adhesive felt and a small center square of adhesive foam. Intermediate spaces were then printed with a smaller frame-shaped unit, also of adhesive felt.

90

• Cardboard cannisters covered with
printed brown paper.

PORTFOLIO

A portfolio is a handy place to store magazine clippings, photographs, or artwork. Print the cover of a portfolio or cover it with a hand-printed paper. Fabric tape binds the two covers at the seam, and a shoelace tie holds them together at the top.

   The pattern used in the illustration is a four-way branching design, with the foam stems reaching all four edges of the cardboard printing block in such a way that the ends of these stems seem to join with those of adjoining prints. Detailing is added to the leaf shapes in the foam by dotting them with white glue. The glue dots, when dry, print as dark spots surrounded by white rings.

Materials
adhesive foam, 1 sheet
wooden or cardboard block, 3 inches
     (7.62 cm) square
stamp pad and ink, black
scissors
fine-line felt marker
compass or large pin
toothpick
white glue
ruler
pencil
2 sheets of tagboard, 16 by 18 inches
     (40.64 by 45.72 cm)
fabric tape, black
single-edged razor blade or artist's knife
shoelace, black

Instructions
1. Use the felt marker to draw the design illustrated or one of your own on the square of adhesive foam. Each stem line touching the margin on one edge of the printing block must have a corresponding stem line touching it at the same point on the opposite edge. This must also be true for the points at which stem lines touch the top or bottom edges of the block.
2. With scissors, cut the design from the piece of foam. Using the point of a compass or pin to catch the center of the plastic, peel the protective covering from the back, taking care not to tear the foam.
3. Position the adhesive foam design on the block of wood and press it firmly in place. Draw an arrow on the back of the wood block to indicate the top of the design. This will help eliminate misprints.
4. Dip a toothpick in white glue to make a dot of glue on each of the leaf shapes in the design. Let dry.
5. Using a ruler and pencil, draw a light grid of 3-inch (7.62-cm) squares on the colored side of the tagboard sheets.
6. Ink the printing block by pressing it several times on a saturated stamp pad. Print in each penciled square on the tagboard, reinking for each print.

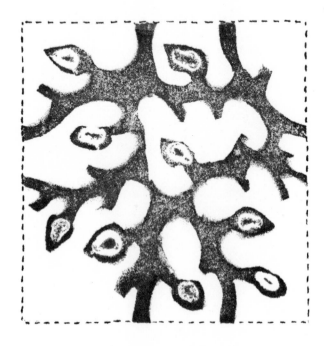

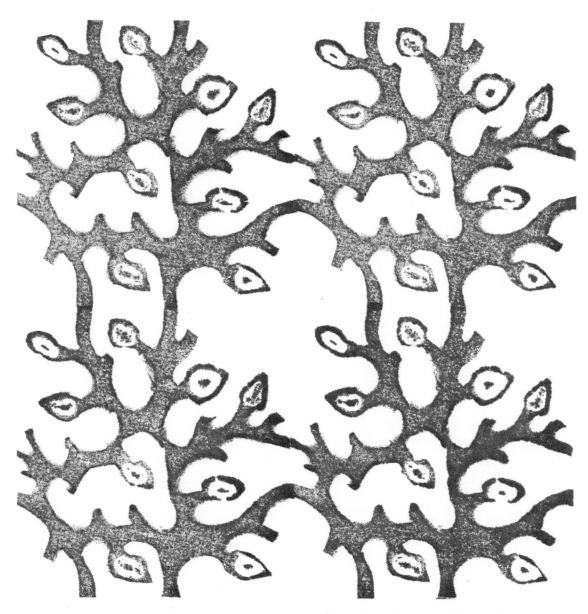

• A cardboard printing block with a design cut from adhesive foam created this simple branching pattern. Dried dots of white glue on the foam alter the printing surface of the leaf shapes.

7. Fasten the two sheets of tagboard together, printed sides out, with a strip of black tape along the seam. Fold the two sheets open and tape the inside of the seam as well. Tape the four exposed corners, folding the tape inward and trimming the edges on the diagonal with a single-edged razor blade or artist's knife.

8. With the razor blade or artist's knife cut a slit near the top center margin of each sheet of tagboard. Thread one end of a black shoelace through each slit, using a compass point to press it through if needed. Tape one end of the shoelace securely against the inside of the tagboard cover. Cut the celluloid tip off the other end.

• **A tagboard portfolio printed with a simple branching pattern.**

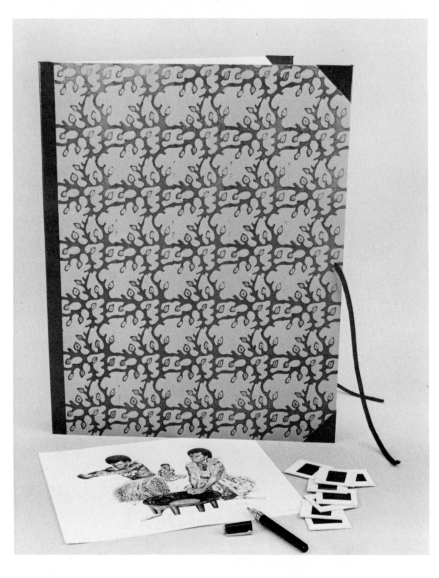

POTHOLDER

Many of your designs will suggest use on fabric. Test both a design and a printing method on a small project such as potholders or pillow covers. The most successful ideas can later be used for quilts or garments in your own original patterns. Any stiffness in the printed areas of the fabric will disappear after it has been washed a time or two.

Adhesive foam works well with oil-based printer's ink (from a shop selling artists' supplies for printing small fabric projects). The foam may begin to pucker and tear when used for printing an expanse of yardage, but if this happens, a second printing block can be made to finish the project. To do this, print the design on a clean sheet of foam, then on a clean block of wood. Carefully cut out the foam design and glue it onto the wood, using the printed image on the wood as a guide for placement. The resulting printing block should reproduce the same design as the one it replaced.

Materials

adhesive foam, one sheet
3 soft corn pads
wooden block, 4 inches (10.16 cm) square
oil-based printer's ink, red
scissors
plastic cloth
masking tape
sheet of glass, about 12 inches (30.48 cm) square
soft gelatin brayer
lightweight muslin, prewashed, ⅓ yard (30.48 cm)
paint thinner
paper towels
newsprint
iron
pressing cloth
white vinegar
water
cotton quilt batting
fabric piping, 1 yard (91.44 cm), red
bias tape, 6 inches (15.24 cm), red
thread to match muslin

Instructions

1. Use scissors to cut four narrow strips of adhesive foam. Cut one strip into ten small squares. Arrange the foam pieces and the corn pads on the wood block in the design illustrated or in a design of your own. Press the foam firmly to the block to make it adhere. (White glue should be used on the blocks for printing a large project.)

2. Protect your work surface with a plastic cloth. Use small pieces of masking tape to fasten the four corners of a 7-inch-square (17.8-cm-square) piece of muslin to the work surface.

3. Squeeze a small amount of printer's ink onto the sheet of glass. Spread it into a thin uniform layer by rolling the brayer back and forth over it.

4. When the brayer is covered with ink, roll it across the foam on the block to coat it evenly with color.

5. Position the block carefully in one corner of the muslin, leaving ½-inch (1.27-cm) seam allowance along each edge, with the corn pads toward the center of the square piece of fabric. Lean on it with both hands to make a good print. Print the other three corner sections of the muslin in the same way, reinking for each print. To print a companion pattern for a second potholder, print each of the blocks with the corn pad corner of the design turned outward. Clean the brayer and glass with paint thinner and paper towels.

6. Hang the printed fabric in an out-of-the-way spot to dry for several days. To set the ink and ensure the pot-

holder's washability, cover the ironing board with a piece of newsprint and lay the printed fabric facedown on it. Iron it slowly and thoroughly with a dry iron set at medium temperature. After the ink has been heat-set, iron it again using a pressing cloth dampened with a mixture of white vinegar and water. Fold the ½-inch (1.27-cm) seam allowance under and press it flat.

7. Sandwich the piece of batting between printed and unprinted fabric squares. Arrange the piping between the two folded edges and baste the three together. Fold the piece of bias tape in half, insert the ends at one corner of the potholder, and baste it in place.

8. Machine- or hand-stitch around the printed design and then around the seam.

• Potholders printed with an adhesive foam design, using oil-based printer's ink.

• Prints made with a wooden block, adhesive foam strips, and corn pads arranged in four-step rotation.

CHAPTER EIGHT
Sponge prints

Sponges, both natural and cellulose, are available in many shapes and sizes. Natural sea sponge, cut by machine into smooth blocks, is sold with household cleaning supplies. It has a slightly better printing surface than cellulose, is a little easier to carve, and is sometimes sold in a perfect-to-hold humpback shape. Although artificial sponges are not quite as nice to work with, they too will make a good print. The large block sponges of either kind can be used to print patterns on walls and floors. The carving is done with a very sharp single-edged razor blade. Do not try to cut sponge with a used blade or you will have a lot of ragged edges. You may need to use more than one blade to carve a single sponge design.

To plan a large-scale pattern, carve gum erasers and develop a small pattern using stamp pad and paper. When you have completed a design that pleases you, simply enlarge it and carve it on the flat surface of the sponge. Then print your wall or floor with acrylic or flat latex paint. If you want a glossy look, paint the finished pattern with liquid plastic.

The design possibilities are endless, and an intricate pattern can be printed as quickly as a simple one once the sponge has been carved. When a basic pattern has been established on a floor or wall, it is easy to make it more complex by adding details to the pattern with a smaller carved sponge or eraser and a second or even third color.

Some smaller sponges print effectively on paper, though they may need to be stamped twice to get a good print. Sponges are often used to print an under-

• **A basic pattern made with the sponge top of a stamp-moistening jar.**

• **Curved cuts were made in a sponge for a scale pattern.**

• Pattern of small whole and half-cut sponge prints built over compass-penciled circles; pencil eraser prints and felt marker detailing added.

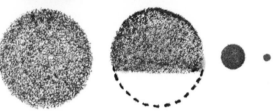

glaze pattern on greenware. Ceramic shops sell small sponges in a variety of shapes for this purpose, or you can cut your own.

DECORATED PLATE

Greenware plates are easy to decorate with sponges and underglaze in any color you like. The ceramic studio will then fire the plate for you and will refire it after you have given it two coats of clear overglaze. The heavy plates have the bright appeal of folk art, and once you start printing you will find it very easy to begin thinking of decorating whole breakfast sets in your favorite colors, each plate an original design. Besides being attractive, inexpensive, and easy to do, the finished plates are dishwasher safe.

Materials
3 stamp-moistening jars with sponge tops
pencil with eraser
typewriter eraser
3 small jars of translucent underglaze,
    blue, light green, and dark green
single-edged razor blade
greenware plate
scrub cloth
compass
masking tape
water, small amount
aluminum foil
very small watercolor paintbrush
wide, flat watercolor paintbrush
overglaze, clear

Instructions
1. Use a single-edged razor blade to cut one of the sponges in half. Follow the circular design illustrated or create one of your own. The instructions given here are for the plate on the left side of the illustration.
2. Wipe the plate with a barely damp cloth. Handle the plate very carefully, as greenware is fragile.
3. Use the compass to draw three concentric circles on the plate. Make the central circle 1¼ inches (3.18 cm) in

• **Whole and half-cut sponge and typewriter eraser prints in a circular arrangement; detailing added with a felt marker.**

diameter, the next circle 2½ inches (6.35 cm) in diameter, and the outermost circle 3¾ inches (9.54 cm) in diameter.
4. Divide the area between the central circle and the next circle into eighths. Draw penciled lines that divide the area in half, then in fourths, then in eighths. Round off the outer corners of each of these sections to outline the eight petal shapes.

• **Ceramic plates with a sponge print pattern in underglaze.**

5. Mix a small amount of blue underglaze with a few drops of water on a piece of aluminum foil. The underglaze should be the consistency of milk. Pour a small pool of each of the other colors on the piece of foil, adding some water to each.
6. Pat the uncut sponge in the light green underglaze to ink it, then print it lightly in the center of the plate. Ink the cut sponge in light green to print the half-circle shapes in the design.
7. Using a very small brush, paint the two centermost penciled circular out-

lines with underglaze in blue. Paint blue stem lines between the half-circle prints and thin blue leaves curved to follow the shape of the print.
8. Use the small brush to outline the eight petal shapes in dark green and a typewriter eraser to print a dark green dot at the end of each stem line.
9. Repeat the border, if you wish, around the edge of the plate.
10. Have the plate fired at the ceramic studio. Using the wide brush, paint it with two coats of overglaze in thick, flowing strokes, allowing drying time between coats. Have the plate refired. (Dilute the overglaze with water for the first coat if this is recommended in the manufacturer's instructions.)

101

PRINTED WALL BASKETWEAVE PATTERN

A sponge-printed pattern is most easily done on a wall unbroken by doors or windows. The wall should be painted with a base coat of washable flat latex. Almost any kind of pattern can be carved in the sponge by using a very sharp blade. Cuts need not be deep and should be slanted toward each other, undercutting the area to be removed. For the walls illustrated, a double cross-band design was carved in a rectangular sponge so that two design units were printed with each stamp of the sponge. Natural sea sponges sold in blocks with humpback shapes are the easiest to handle and are worth looking for.

A few lightly penciled guidelines drawn across the wall at intervals will help keep the rows of prints from going up- or downhill. A second sponge can be printed, carved to match the first, and then cut to fit partial spaces, should they occur at corners or casements. Misprints should be washed off immediately, and minor corrections can be made later by painting out mistakes with some of the base coat color. Strips of masking tape protect adjoining walls and ceiling, and newspapers protect the floor.

Materials
2 large sponges, rectangular or hump-
    backed
1 pint washable flat latex, mustard color
single-edged razor blade
indelible felt marker
pencil
yardstick
water, small amount
masking tape
newspapers
flat paint tray
wide, flat paintbrush
large sheets of newsprint
ladder
scrub cloth
warm, soapy water

Instructions
1. Use a single-edged razor blade to carve one of the sponges in a basket-weave design or create a design of your own. If your sponge is twice as long as it is wide, carve two square design units on its surface, side by side. For each of the units, cut a small triangular piece from each of the four sides. The tip of each triangle should align over the midpoint of each side and should point toward the center of the unit. Cut a diagonal strip from the lower left corner to the upper right corner of the unit on the left, leaving an uncut portion between the strip and the triangle. Cut another strip from the lower right corner to the upper left corner in the other unit. Cut a short strip from the outside upper corner of each unit, stopping just short of the center. Do the same from the two lower inside corners. Use a felt marker to draw an arrow on the back of the sponge, indicating which side is to be printed up.
2. Draw a few parallel guidelines at intervals across the wall, using a pencil and yardstick. Keep the lines light so that they can be easily washed off later.
3. Dampen the sponge and squeeze it dry.
4. Pour a small amount of latex paint in the tray. Use the flat brush to spread it evenly over the bottom of the pan. Pat the carved sponge over the layer of paint to ink it. Print a sample pattern on newsprint to determine the amount of paint and pressure needed to make a clear image.

• This cross-band pattern was printed with a thin layer of cut sponge mounted on a wooden block.

• **Walls printed with latex paint in a cross-band pattern using a large carved sponge.**

5. Beginning at the top corner of the wall in the most visible corner of the room, print the carved sponge several times before reinking. After part of the wall has been printed, stand back from it to see if any of the prints are noticeably lighter than the rest. Reprint any that seem to need it, being very careful to stamp the sponge in exactly the same location on the wall. A slightly uneven look is part of the appeal of a hand-printed pattern, so keep corrections to a minimum.

6. If there is not enough room for a row of complete prints at the far margin of the wall or at the baseboard, use the sponge to print the complete design unit on the second sponge, then carve the portion needed to fit the partial spaces.

CHAPTER NINE

Soft plastic prints

Soft plastic modeling compound such as Plast • i • clay or Eveready is the non-hardening clay used in kindergartens. It is an extremely versatile printing medium and can be reused endless times. The plastic itself can be shaped and used as a stamp for printing, or it can be flattened, cut, and glued to a cardboard or wood printing block. It can also be incised, indented, or used to take impressions that will print.

The softness of the material does put some limitations on it. It usually prints best over a felt-padded work surface and does not hold its shape for extensive stamping. Its best use, therefore, is in printing one good design to be photocopied for such things as notecards, posters, or gift tags.

Soft plastic can be flattened by pounding it with a hammer, then rolling it with a rolling pin on a smooth surface. In-cised or indented lines are most easily removed from the plastic surface by scraping with a single-edged razor blade, then pressing the scraped side down on a smooth surface.

• **Use a hammer or rolling pin to flatten soft plastic modeling compound.**

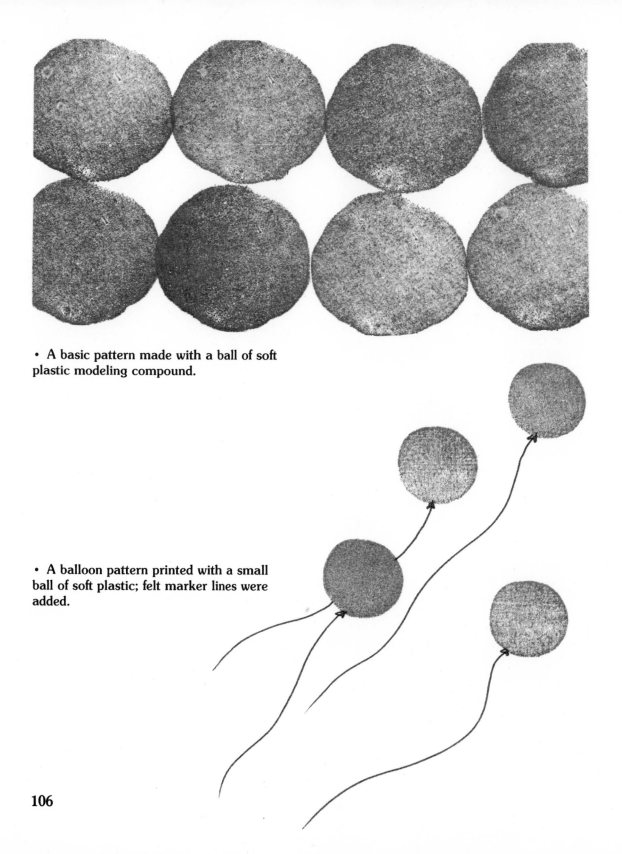

• A basic pattern made with a ball of soft plastic modeling compound.

• A balloon pattern printed with a small ball of soft plastic; felt marker lines were added.

• Textured pattern, printed with a small cube of soft plastic which had been pressed on a sisal rug.

• A thick cube of soft plastic was pressed down on a smooth surface, then on a piece of fern, then printed over a padded work surface. Felt marker lines created the background. This pattern would work well on matching gift wrap and tags.

108

• A ball of soft plastic was pressed against the design on a Mexican ashtray to create the face in this pattern. The sun's rays were printed with a spoon handle impression on a strip of soft plastic.

• A smooth ball of soft plastic was pressed
flat on one side, then pressed down on the
back side of a heavily veined wild lilac leaf
to pick up its impression. The design was
constructed from the center outward and a
felt marker background and borders were
added.

• A piece of soft plastic was pinched into a fish shape, then flattened on one side. Indentations were made in the smooth surface with the edge of a jar top, a pen cap, and a compass point. A pencil eraser indentation prints as an eye socket. The same eraser is used to print the dark eyes in the finished pattern.

• Soft plastic, flattened with a rolling pin and cut into shapes, made this print. The bird and branch shapes were fastened with white glue to a cardboard printing block. Detailing was added with the point of a compass and the bird's eye was made with the recessed tip of a ball-point pen. A print was taken by laying paper over the inked plastic and rubbing it carefully with the fingers.

ADDRESS BOOK

An address book, covered in black and decorated with a hand-printed design, can be an attractive and inexpensive gift. It will be especially appreciated if it already contains neatly copied addresses from the recipient's old book. Personalize the design if you like, using a fish motif for the fisherman or an orchid for a hothouse gardener.

• A print made with soft plastic rolled flat, then cut into desired shapes and glued onto a square of a cardboard. Lines were incised in the clay with a compass point. A print was then taken by laying a sheet of paper on the inked soft plastic and rubbing it with the fingers.

Materials

soft plastic modeling compound
large stamp pad and ink, black
cardboard
scissors
mimeograph paper
pencil
hammer
rolling pin
aluminum foil
compass or large pin
artist's knife
white glue
large spoon
lightweight fadeproof art paper, black
spray adhesive

Instructions

1. Cut a piece of mimeograph paper slightly smaller than the front of the address book. On it sketch the design illustrated or create one of your own.
2. Hammer and roll the soft plastic flat on a piece of aluminum foil. Turn it over so that the smooth side is up. Lay the sketch on it, faceup, and trace over the main lines, using enough pressure to mark the plastic surface beneath it. Remove the paper and use a compass point to draw in the details.
3. With the artist's knife, cut the design from the plastic. Spread a very thin layer of white glue on the cardboard piece and position the plastic design on it. When the glue has dried, turn the printing block over and press it on a smooth surface to flatten any distortions caused by the cutting.
4. To ink the block, lay it facedown on a well-saturated stamp pad and burnish the back with a large spoon. Take care not to press it down over the metal rim of the stamp pad box. Turn the block over to see if it is completely inked. Lay a sheet of mimeo-

113

graph paper on the inked block, holding it in place with one hand. Rub the paper gently with the fingers of the other hand, making sure all parts are printed. Peel the paper from the block and examine the print. Make any corrections needed in the printing block and reprint it.

5. When you have made a successful print, hand-letter it (or use a child's printing set) with the word *Addresses.*
6. Trim the print to a size slightly smaller than the address book cover.
7. Cut a piece of black fadeproof art paper large enough to cover the address book with ½-inch (1.27 cm) allow-

ance to be folded inside. Cut two endpapers to fit the inside of the front and back covers. Spray the back of the papers with adhesive. Wrap the large piece around the address book, folding the edges inside. Press the endpapers in place to cover those edges.
8. Spray the back of the print design with adhesive and center it on the book cover, pressing it firmly in place.

• **A covered address book decorated with a print made from soft plastic.**

HOLIDAY GREETING CARD

Cookie cutter shapes cut from soft plastic modeling compound, then incised and embellished, can form the basic design for holiday cards. A horse shape, for example, needs only a rocker and a sky of polka-dot stars to give the feeling of Christmas. Other shapes will suggest other holidays— a heart-shaped cookie cutter for red valentine prints or a shamrock for all the O'Reillys you know. If you need a shape you do not have in your kitchen drawer, roll out the plastic and cut it with the pointed blade of an artist's (X-acto) knife.

In this design a horse cookie cutter was used, with strips of soft plastic added to the printing block for a rocker, tail, and borders. Detailing was cut into the plastic surface with a compass point, and the lid of a pen made the polka-dot pattern. Dots in the background were added to the completed print with a typewriter eraser.

• **A print made with soft plastic rolled flat and cut with a cookie cutter. The horse shape was glued to a cardboard printing block, indented and incised, and then inked and printed. Typewriter eraser dots add to the finished design.**

115

The design, printed on mimeograph paper, was then run through a photocopying machine, with those copies cut out to be mounted on note cards.

Materials
soft plastic modeling compound
typewriter eraser
cardboard
large stamp pad and ink, black
horse-shaped cookie cutter
ruler
scissors
aluminum foil
hammer
rolling pin
kitchen knife
white glue
compass or large pin
pen cap
ball-point pen
large spoon
mimeograph paper (typing paper will do)
white note cards with matching envelopes

Instructions
1. Cut a piece of cardboard 6 inches (15.24 cm) square for the design illustrated, or in a size to fit a design of your own.
2. Flatten some soft plastic on a piece of aluminum foil by pounding it with a hammer, then rolling it into a smooth sheet with a rolling pin.
3. Use the cookie cutter to cut a horse-shaped piece from the sheet of soft plastic, and with a knife, cut some strips ¼ inch (6.35 mm) wide to be used as the rocker and borders. Cut a piece for the tail, then carefully peel away the foil, taking care not to distort the shapes of the soft plastic pieces.
4. Arrange the soft plastic shapes on the piece of cardboard, facedown, and attach them with a little white glue. Use the point of a compass to incise lines in the horse shape to indicate hair in the mane and tail, and parts of the bridle and saddle blanket. Incise a line along the rocker and on the borders. Use the end of a pen cap to press in the dapple design on the horse and a ball-point pen with the tip recessed to make the horse's eye and the dots on the borders.
5. Ink the cardboard and plastic block by laying it facedown on a well-saturated stamp pad. Burnish the back of the cardboard with the round part of a large spoon. Do not press down on any part of the block that extends over the metal edge of the stamp pad container. Move any overlapping part of the block to the center of the pad before burnishing it.
6. Turn the block over to see if it is completely inked. If it is not, reink the pad and repeat the process.
7. Lay a piece of mimeograph paper over the inked soft plastic, holding it in place with one hand and rubbing the paper with the fingers of the other hand. Peel the paper from the printing block and set it aside while you print others. Minor corrections can be made by filling in unwanted white spaces. Ink a typewriter eraser and use it to print any spots that were missed. Typewriter correction fluid can be used to cover smudges.
8. Run the best print through a photocopying machine to make as many copies as you need for your greeting cards. Trim the design to fit the notecards, spray adhesive on the back, and press them in place. Envelopes can be printed with typewriter eraser dots on the inside of the flap.

• **A cookie cutter and soft plastic were used to create the design for these greeting cards.**

CHAPTER TEN

Miscellaneous prints

You will find that much of your enjoyment in stamp pad printing comes from finding new materials with which to print. Watch for items with interesting shapes, but do not overlook something as simple as a rubber drain plug. The rings that it will print can form many patterns to be embellished with other prints. Keep plugs and spools on hand in different sizes, available to be used either as the basic design unit in a pattern or to provide a detail in whatever size is needed.

• A pencil tube, designed to keep pencils from rolling, makes an interesting stamp.

• Use your imagination and print with common household items, such as a knitting needle guard.

• Use a spool of thread—the type with holes that radiate from the center—for making prints.

• The simulated footprint is an old-time children's favorite. It is stamped with the side of a clenched fist. The "toes" are printed with the tip of one finger.

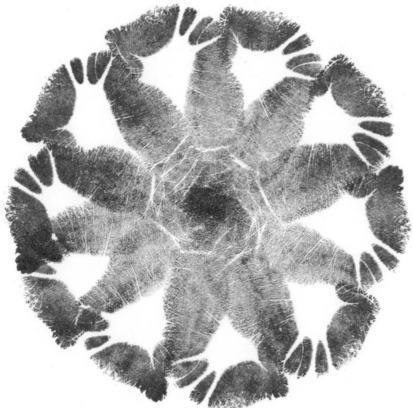

• **A flower of fist prints, made by rotating the paper as a child's fist is stamped repeatedly in the same position.**

Some possible stamps, such as rubber washers, have nice printing surfaces but are not easy to hold. Glue one to a bottle cap or arrange several on a larger bottle top for easy handling.

Most rubber or resilient plastic will give a good print. Try printing rubber mats or tennis shoe soles over a paper stencil. Print with a tube that is sold to keep a pencil from rolling or with a knitting needle guard.

Metal and glass items also can make clear prints when used on a padded work surface. A layer or two of felt will provide the resilience lacking in these materials.

A crumpled paper towel printed over stencils gives an interesting effect. Experiment with sandpaper and with plastic scouring pads to vary the textures in similar uses.

Arrange alphabet soup letters to spell out the words of a greeting or your name. Spread a thin layer of white glue on a piece of wood or cardboard and press it down on the letter arrangement. The letters will then be picked up in reverse order—just what you need to print them correctly. When they have dried in place, rub them gently over sandpaper to provide a smooth inking surface.

Stretch a piece of scrap lace over the bottom of a small box, then make prints with it, or over a jar top for printing a patterned round shape. Keep watching for new materials and keep samples of the best ones near your work area.

Do not overlook the use of commercial rubber stamps in your patterns. Remember too that you can splurge on commercially made stamps of your own design. For a very special project you may want a design that is too intricate to be carved in simple materials. When this is the case, draw the design on paper with black ink, check the yellow pages of your phone book for rubber stamp businesses, and have your own design custom-made into a stamp. Use it with stamp pad ink, with oil-based printer's ink for fabric, or with acrylic paint for printing walls.

• The end of a pencil tube was printed in rows as the basis for this pattern. One side of the tube was cut away with a single-edged razor blade to create the prints in the top row of each group. The resulting prints suggested leaves, and flowers on stems were added with a typewriter eraser and felt pen. Other felt pen lines filled in spaces between rows of prints and pencil eraser prints were added.

• Cotton string glued in a spiral on a wooden block was used to print this pattern.

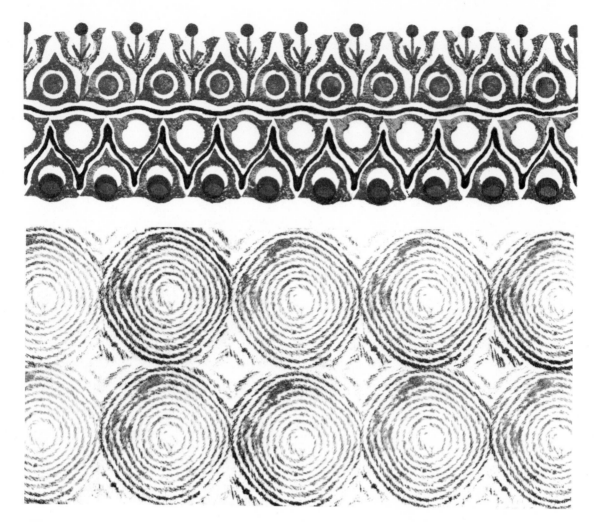

• A stencil project for Halloween, printed with a crumpled paper towel over cut-paper shapes. Using a crumpled paper towel as the stamp, the background is printed first, with a round piece of paper held in place to block out a moon. That paper is removed and a second stencil, with the lower edge cut as the silhouette of rooftops, is used to cover the upper two-thirds of the picture, the middle ground. After this area is printed with the paper towel, the stencil is removed. The third and last stencil is a sheet of paper from which the trees and foreground have been cut.

• A commercial stamp, Black Bear (© Nature Impressions), used with carved vinyl eraser prints and felt marker stripes. Commercially made rubber stamps are sold in many gift shops, stationery shops, and toy stores.

• A pattern (opposite page) designed by tracing the branching lines in the pattern on page 17 and adding a few extra leaves and flowers. The resulting felt marker drawing was then taken to a rubber stamp company, where it was reduced in size before being

made into a stamp. This stamp can be used
as an all-over pattern for gift wrap, combined with a geometric print in vertical
stripes, or printed as a border for stationery.
Children's drawings can also be made into
rubber stamps and make charming
Christmas cards or can be used on fabric
with printer's ink.

123

• Paper punch dots of sheet rubber were
glued to a wooden block and printed. Typewriter eraser prints were added for accent.

COASTERS

Hand-printed designs to be used as coasters can be commercially laminated at very little cost. Look in your phone directory to see if your community has a lamination business. The coasters shown here were printed with the end of a spool of thread, then colored with felt markers before they were laminated. A different combination of colors was used in each coaster. Lamination can also be used on hand-printed placemats for holiday breakfasts.

• **Prints made with two spools of thread, a carved pencil eraser, and a typewriter eraser. Ink the end of a spool with a twisting motion and print it over a lightly padded work surface.**

Materials
2 spools of thread, one larger than the other
pencil eraser
typewriter eraser
stamp pad and ink, black
single-edged razor blade
typing or mimeograph paper
small piece of felt or other soft fabric
indelible felt markers, assorted colors
white glue
paper punch
compass

Instructions
1. Use a single-edged razor blade to carve the pencil eraser in a teardrop shape in order to use the design illustrated or create a design of your own.
2. Remove the paper from one end of the large spool, ink it on the stamp pad, and print it on a sheet of typing paper. A piece of felt or other cushioning might be needed under the paper to get a clear print.
3. Ink the end of the smaller spool and print it above, below, and at each side of the larger print, taking care to place the prints directly opposite one another, with each touching the edge of the center print. Add another small spool print in each of the remaining spaces around the large print.
4. With the uncut pencil eraser, print a dot in the center of the design. Print typewriter eraser dots in the centers of the smaller spool prints. Use the carved pencil eraser to put a teardrop-shaped print in each of the spaces between the spokes of the center print. Print other teardrop shapes at each of the creases in the scalloped outer margin.
5. Repeat the process to print as many coaster designs as you need. Color them with felt markers and glue a white paper punch dot in the center of each.
6. Cut out the designs and have them commercially laminated.

• Laminated coasters of brightly colored
spool-print patterns.

Index